FINAL TOUR OF

NORTH AMERICAN'S T-28 TROJANS

ROBERT GENAT

In memory of Craig Morrison

Published by:
Specialty Press Publishers and Wholesalers
11481 Kost Dam Road
North Branch, MN 55056
612/583-3239

Printed in Hong Kong

Designed by Greg Compton

ISBN
0-933424-61-2

TABLE OF CONTENTS

NORTH AMERICAN'S T-28 TROJANS

THE SECRET OF THE T-28

If I were to ask the average aviation enthusiast to name the one propeller-driven trainer that can outclimb and outturn a P-51, I'm sure I'd get back a puzzled look and some vigorous head scratches. Then I'd hear a nervous laugh followed by, "Is this a trick question?" Then I'd ask: "Which propeller-driven aircraft performed a close air-support role in conflicts worldwide? Which propeller-driven aircraft carried one particular pilot on more than 5,000 combat missions?"

More head scratching and more shifting from foot to foot. Then I'd deliver my coup de grâce: "Which propeller-driven warbird is the best-flying and the funnest aircraft ever built, as confirmed by hundreds of veteran military aviators? Corsair? Mustang? Bearcat?"

No, no and no. The correct answer is the North American T-28.

"That stocky, blunt-nosed machine that leaked oil all over the place and trained thousands of Air Force and Navy pilots?" the enthusiast might ask. That's right, Mr. Enthusiast; you got it right, but not entire-

ly. The Air Force and Navy certainly used T-28s to train pilots, but most T-28s don't have to leak now. That's just one of the more fascinating stories about this superb aircraft.

The T-28 is arguably the best-kept secret in aviation. Perched on the ground, high on its tricycle gear, it looks ungainly because of its big cowlings, loping, noisy engines and that bulging, two-piece canopy. Awkward as it appears on the ground, in the air it is beautiful. The more you're around T-28s, the better they get.

The T-28 is a true, dual-control aircraft with virtually identical front and rear cockpits that both offer excellent visibility. Unlike many World War II fighters that were modified to include rear seats, the T-28's rear cockpit is roomy. And, the T-28 may be the most complex of the propeller-driven warbirds around, but it is also one of the easiest to maintain. Of special interest to former Navy guys like me: Some T-28s even come with tailhooks.

Nearly twenty years ago, I was introduced to this fascinating aircraft. My earliest T-28 recollection is from my own days in the Navy in the mid-sixties. I was assigned to an S2F squadron, and our base had a hack T-28. Every base back then seemed to have a T-28 for the use of its commanding officer and other command-level officers to maintain their flying proficiency, as well as provide them with a fun method of transportation. At the time, I knew the T-28 was a trainer with the same big radial engine as our Stoofs, but beyond that, I knew very little about the T-28. Then in the mid-eighties, I noticed that the T-28 was beginning to appear at air shows in increasing numbers, sporting many different color schemes and markings; restorers can choose color schemes from nearly all U.S. forces and from many in other countries.

Media freeloader that I am, I always try to catch rides at air shows. At a warbird show in San Diego in 1986, I was going through my usual begging routines, undaunted by owners' refusals to let a journalist so much as set foot in their prize aircraft. Then I came upon a white T-28 that the owner was spit-shining. I went through the usual photographer rap, ending with my big finish, "If you have an open seat, I'd like to fly with you today." "Sure," he said. He did have an open seat, and he let me ride. I couldn't believe it. Me, a complete stranger and a media weenie to boot! During the idle time before take-off, we got to know each other, and I questioned him about his plane.

On that flight, I discovered what a gem the T-28 was. That owner became a good friend of mine, and during the next few years, we traveled to a number of air shows, including Oshkosh. I met several other T-28 owners, got in a little stick time and realized why this unlikely aircraft was becoming such a popular warbird. For the past few years, I have flown in, photographed and thrown up in some of the finest examples of this type. I hope your journey through this book will be as pleasant and enlightening for you as was my time with today's T-28 owners, pilots and restorers.

—*Robert Genat*

Robert Genat is a San Diego photographer who specializes in military, aviation, automotive and law enforcement topics. He has been interested in aviation since he saw his first contrail across the skies of Michigan at the age of two, and he has been interested in warbirds since he conducted his own heroic dog fights in the basement of the family home in Detroit. The smell of aviation fuel is merely a substitute for model airplane glue.

WHAT MAKES THE T-28 SO SPECIAL?

The T-28 is not a well-known aircraft. World War II's Mustangs, Hellcats and Corsairs are the definitive warbird icons. They helped win the last war that was strongly supported by all Americans, and their pilots were glamorized by John Wayne and other Hollywood heroes of that era.

The T-28's historic niche, however, is a whole lot different. First, the T-28 was designed solely as a trainer, and is about as unglamorous and functional as my dad's four-door Chevy with its stick six. I learned to drive in that Chevy, but the car I really wanted was a bright red Corvette. Like my dad's Chevy, trainers are meant to be functional. All beginner pilots learned their basics in a trainer before they were allowed to jump into the cockpit of an F-86 or F9F.

Four T-28s sit forlornly at the Davis-Monthan Air Force storage facility in the Arizona desert. Without an engine, the aircraft requires a support under its rear fuselage to prevent it from tipping backward. The base's dry climate along with the use of proper preservation techniques have given today's warbird owners a source of excellent core airframes for restorations.

Later, in Southeast Asia, those T-28s that qualified for warbird status participated in one of America's must unpopular wars but received little notice. News footage from Indochina focused on F-4s and B-52s and their state-of-the-art electronics, missiles and bombs. At a time when politicians were arguing about dropping nuclear weapons on the enemy, describing the success of a functional, single-engine propeller airplane would have been bad PR. Besides, much of the information on the early success of the T-28 in Vietnam was classified, making it even more unlikely that anyone would learn of its warbird status. Only recently has information become

The Beechcraft T-34 replaced the T-28 as the Navy's primary trainer, and the turbo version of the T-34 is still used by the Navy today. (photo Joe Cupido)

available concerning the T-28's role in forward air control in Southeast Asia, as well as those maverick T-28 pilots known as The Ravens.

Technically, the T-28 was the most advanced propeller-driven military aircraft ever designed. It was built by North American Aviation, a company that had years of experience with its successful designs for the P-51, T-6, B-25 and F-86. North American-

NORTH AMERICAN'S T-28 TROJANS

A gray T-28 bathes in the pink glow of a setting sun.

built aircraft had been tested in the toughest laboratory available: war. North American's engineers knew how an airplane should fly and how it should be maintained, and they built five models of the T-28—the A, B, C and D models and the Fennec—and several variants.

In 1948, the Air Force chose North American to build its new training aircraft, which would simulate a jet's performance. Late the next year, the first prototype flew, and the Air Force ordered 266 T-28A Trojans, which featured tandem seating, dual controls, an 800 HP Wright Cyclone engine, a two-blade propeller and a tricycle landing gear with a steerable nose wheel. The A was used by the Air Force from 1950 to 1956 and went through several minor modifications. After the model was shelved by the Air Force, T-28As served in the National Guard and in a few foreign wars or they were stored at a military base in Arizona.

In 1952, the Navy created the T-28B when it asked North American to modify the T-28A to contain a larger 1425 HP engine and add a three-blade propeller and an under-fuselage speed brake. From 1954 to 1955, 489 T-28Bs rolled off the production line. The Navy used Bs as trainers, base hacks, test planes, drone controllers and observation planes. It also saw action in Southeast Asia and served in a non-military hail and thunderstorm study and as a firefighter.

The C model was essentially a B model that was adjusted to handle aircraft carrier landings for the Navy. The modifications included the addition of a tailhook, a strengthened airframe and a smaller propeller. From 1955 to 1957 North American produced 299 T-28Cs and converted a few As and Bs

FINAL TOUR OF DUTY

into Cs. It was used to teach many pilots the delicacies of aircraft carrier landings.

In late 1959, France requested the next T-28 model, the Fennec, designated the T-28S by France and T-28F by the United States. Frustrated in its efforts to acquire T-28Bs, which were claimed by the Navy, the French hired Pacific Airmotive to modify T-28As to their specifications, which included a larger engine, a three-bladed propeller, an airscoop, and additional armament capabilities and armor. From 1961 to 1962, Fennecs flew combat in Algeria. After the action, many went back to France for training and reserve use, the rest were sold off to other countries, including Morocco and Argentina.

The T-28D-5 and T-28D-10, also known as the Tango or the AT-28 (attack), were built for combat in Southeast Asia. Initially rebuilt from A-model airframes, North American converted 191 T-28Ds and Fairchild Aviation converted 50, later modifying 72 B models into Ds. The T-28D featured the 1820 HP engine, B/C

Propeller blades blur as this 1820 radial engine is turned up. The intake scoop at the top, front edge of the cowling is a carburetor intake.

Formation flying in a T-28 doesn't get much better than that seen in this "fingertip" formation. When flown properly, it's a beautiful sight.

cowlings, armor plate, self-sealing fuel tanks, stronger wing spars and the extraction seat. The D was used by the United States in Laos and Vietnam during combat and later by foreign countries' military forces, including the Royal Laotian Air Force.

All the T-28 models share many appealing characteristics, but the T-28's maintainability is one of its best features. All of its systems can be easily reached from ground level. The battery is located in the side of the fuselage and has three fasteners on its access door. The battery-access door is hinged at the bottom, so the battery slides out easily. Near the battery is an external power receptacle. The engine cowlings on both sides open upward and feature internal prop rods to hold them open. Footholds in the flaps and hand-holds in the side of the fuselage provide convenient access to the top of the wing. If the flaps are not retracted, a lever on the left side of the fuselage releases them.

FINAL TOUR OF DUTY

On top of each wing is a standard fuel cap. Accesses to the hydraulic reservoir and oil tank are located on the top left side of the cowling, so the crew chief or plane captain can reach both access doors while standing on the left wing. The reservoirs were placed slightly forward of the leading edge, so North American added a handy pull-out step at the rear edge of the exhaust deflector on the left cowling. Once a crewman is on the wing, he can slide back the canopy. On the left front edge of the rear canopy a fold-down handle allows that canopy to be opened by hand.

Let's have a look at the fuselage. Just aft of the speed brake (on the B, C and D models) is a large baggage door with two latches. The baggage door is large enough for two adults to comfortably access the oxygen bottles, canopy air bottle or the electronic black boxes. On many aircraft, this com-

partment is commonly called the "hell hole" by ground crews because of its tight quarters while performing maintenance. But not in the T-28. Maintenance accessibility is excellent, and its baggage door is truly a baggage door. Unlike the icon

T-28s are often maligned as not being authentic warbirds. The lead aircraft in this formation is a Fennec that was flown in combat in Algeria, and the D model shown is of the type that was flown in Vietnam and Laos confrontations.

The T-6/SNJ was the primary trainer for both the Air Force and the Navy during World War II. (photo J.J. Genat)

FINAL TOUR OF DUTY

warbirds that have only empty wing gun bays available to hold gear, T-28s can carry golf clubs, lawn chairs, even folding bicycles, and the baggage compartment includes a built-in light. The nose-wheel well contains a fold-down ladder that leads to the engine's accessory section and a built-in work light. The T-28 offers eye-level access everywhere with only a screwdriver. How simple can maintenance get?

into the cockpit. Once you're seated, a quick look around confirms that you are in an aircraft designed by North American Aviation. Anyone who has ever flown an F-86 or F-100 will tell you that the cockpit layout is always the same. The T-28 was designed as a transitional trainer, so that design characteristic was intentional.

The instrument panel is well laid-out, and all switches, controls and gauges are back-lit, edge-lit

Let's climb onto the wing and check out the cockpit. Two spring-loaded footholds are located on the left side of the fuselage, one for each seat. The over-size bubble canopy frame means it's a low step-over

When flying the T-28, all you need is a light touch on the stick.

or post-lit. Thunderstorm lights and map lights are standard features that are usually found only on advanced jet fighters and sophisticated airliners.

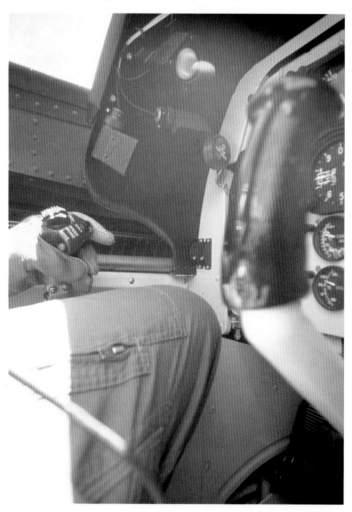

The pedals and seats are adjustable and the shoulder harnesses have locking inertia reels. In the console to the right are electrical, radio, intercom and navigation controls. At its upper end are the primer and starter buttons. Above those, on the lower right of the instrument panel itself, is the magneto switch. Also on that upper right-side console is a switch that makes the T-28 unique: the control shift. This switch shifts all primary electrical controls between the front and rear seats and provides give-and-take control of all systems. The switchable electrical controls include battery, generator, inverters, starter, primer, speed brake and external lighting. The control shift is an unusual and well-engineered feature for a trainer.

What the control shift means for today's civilian owner is the opportunity to get the feel of soloing the T-28 while an experienced pilot rides in the other seat. With duplicate front and rear flight controls, the T-28 can be flown from either seat. When solo flying, however, the pilot is restricted to the front seat, owing to the effect of a single pilot's weight on the aircraft's center of gravity.

Left hand on the throttle. The mike button is for radio communication, the call button is for cockpit interphones. The speed brake switch is on top of the throttle.

FINAL TOUR OF DUTY

Both the best and worst thing about a T-28 is that it's easy to fly. An experienced pilot will enjoy hours of fun in flight. An inexperienced pilot risks being lulled into a false sense of security by the forgiving nature of the trainer.

NORTH AMERICAN'S T-28 TROJANS

In the last decade, the number of T-28s have doubled at Oshkosh. The addition of Clean Kits® and Cleveland brakes have made this airplane an airshow sweetheart.

are on the side of the right-front console and to reach them while strapped-in, the pilot must release the shoulder harness lock, unless he has really long arms.

On the left-hand console in both cockpits are the throttle quadrant and engine controls. The throttle stands almost vertical with three switches positioned for fingertip access while holding the throttle. On top is a slide switch for the speed brake, which switches to two positions: On (deployed) or Off. Two other push switches operate the radio and intercom. Throttle operation is simple: Pushing forward adds power. Just below the throttle is a two-speed supercharger control lever for the engine. When down, the lever engages the high blower; up, the low blower. The illogic of that control (up for low, down for high) is

A few items are found only in the front seat: the control lock that secures flight controls and the throttle on the ground; the parking hand brake located on the lower right of the front instrument panel; and the heater and defroster control and the hand pump for the hydraulic system, both of which are located on the left console. The circuit breakers

FINAL TOUR OF DUTY

If you ever question the heritage of a T-28, take a look at a P-51. The vertical stabilizer fillets on both aircraft are the same, and while the horsepower is also equal, the T-28 will outclimb and outturn a P-51.

NORTH AMERICAN'S T-28 TROJANS

Our intrepid flight leader executes a break. The C model will soon follow.

FINAL TOUR OF DUTY

one of the few design flaws on the T-28.

The throttle quadrant includes the flap control. For easy recognition by touch, it is molded in the shape of an airfoil. Moving the lever activates this hydraulic system: To lower flaps, move the lever down; to retract them, move it up. Detents provide intermediate settings at one-quarter, one-half and three-quarters. The flaps lower hydraulically to a maximum of angle of 37.5 degrees. When the flaps are lowered manually for ground access to the wing, that angle is 50 degrees. A flap-angle indicator is on the instrument panel.

A scene like this takes naval aviators back a few years to a time when the skies over Texas and Florida were filled with trainers.

The next lever in the throttle quadrant is the propeller control, which operates the propeller governor. The final quadrant control adjusts the fuel mixture with three positions: Idle Cutoff, Normal and Rich. Idle Cutoff is the setting used when starting or shutting down the engine. Rich is the setting used for takeoff, climbing, descending, landing and all ground operations, and Normal is the setting used for all other flight operations. Just ahead of the throttle quadrant is the cowl flap and

With the cooperation of the U.S. Navy, a group of T-28Cs flew past the USS Abraham Lincoln *in late 1994.*

FINAL TOUR OF DUTY

This represents the total range of T-28 models manufactured by North American Aviation: A, B, C, D and Fennec. An extremely strong network of owners has evolved.

NORTH AMERICAN'S T-28 TROJANS

oil-cooler-door activator switch.

The cockpit air control is the last lever on the left console. Cockpit ventilation air is gathered from a by-pass in the oil cooler duct. The cockpit has a series of air and defroster outlets. The recommendation is for cockpit air control to remain open at all times, providing constant fresh air, because carbon monoxide is a real peril in the T-28. The engine exhaust runs along the side of the aircraft, past the baggage door. The extended canopy frame and

This is as good as formation flying gets! You could draw a straight line through similar points on each aircraft.

FINAL TOUR OF DUTY

resultant lower pressure in the cockpit can suck carbon monoxide into the cockpit if the seals are not tight. This is one reason not to crack the canopy for "fresh" air; it should always be fully open or fully closed. Fresh air outlets are set at floor and waist levels on either side of both cockpits. Integral with the vent system is an extremely efficient heater.

An engine run-up and propeller check are completed prior to take off. The power of the 1820 Wright Cyclone engine is visible in the compressed front strut.

Aft of the throttle is the canopy control lever, which actuates its hydraulic-powered movement.

NORTH AMERICAN'S T-28 TROJANS

After a short flight, the stainless exhaust deflector is discolored by exhaust deposits. Halfway up the rear edge of this stainless steel panel is a circular object with the word "Step" stenciled nearby. This is a pull-out step for maintenance personnel to check engine oil and hydraulic reservoir. The silver object in the lower right is the exhaust panel for the cockpit heater.

Standard canopy opening takes about three seconds; closing, about six. In an emergency, the canopy can be blown open by an internal high-pressure air bottle, which takes about a half second—another important safety feature. Other warbirds either have cranks or you must pull back on the frame to open their canopies. The sophisticated canopy system on the T-28 equals any jet fighter's.

Below the canopy control on the left console are the trim controls. Trim wheels adjust elevator, rudder and ailerons, and all these controls are easily reached by any pilot, regardless of stature. The seat design provides seven inches of travel, forward and up or rearward and down. With its adjustable rudder pedals, the T-28 offers every pilot a well-designed, efficient "office."

FINAL TOUR OF DUTY

The T-28 features a simple system design that works well. Let's take a look at some of the specific systems.

Fuel System: Each wing contains two interconnected tanks that hold a total of 177 gallons of usable fuel. The cockpit fuel gauge, like that of a jet, indicates pounds of fuel. Fuel from both wings flows by gravity through lines to a fuel sump tank in the right wheel well. When the fuel shut-off valve on the left console is turned on, the electric boost pump starts, opening the fuel shut-off valve. The boost pump maintains a pressure from 19 to 24 PSI. A mechanical pump in the engine provides an operating pressure of 21 to 25 PSI. With some altitude limitations, the engine can operate with one pump.

Speed Brake: Certain World War II aircraft were equipped with dive brakes to control their rates of descent while dive bombing. The last tail dragger manufactured was the Douglas A-1 Skyraider, some of which had dive brakes. When North American engineers first designed the T-28, they incorporated the jet technology of the day and included a speed brake in the T-28 prototype. The brake was rejected by the Air Force for production A models, but it was included on the Navy's B and

Three exhaust pipes per side breathe for the healthy 1425 HP engine.

FINAL TOUR OF DUTY

C models. When A models were modified to D-5s, the speed brake was installed as a bolt-on upgrade on those airframes.

An additional flight control for the pilot, the speed brake can be operated at any airspeed; but a speed of faster than 250 knots causes a pitch-up, which can be counteracted by stick pressure. The speed brake is hydraulically activated by a switch on top of the throttle. The system includes a limiter valve that reduces the possibility of over-stressing the aircraft if the brake deploys at too high a speed. One interesting note: If you are on the ground when a T-28 flies over with its speed brake deployed, you will hear a distinctive whistle that is inaudible from the cockpit.

At idle on the ground, the 1820 engine has the same lope as a top fuel dragster. This engine does not purr, it growls, brimming with power. In flight, the engine sounds as if it's hardly working.

Optional at Extra Cost: The T-28 represents the pinnacle of design for propeller-driven aircraft, but it does have a few minor flaws that once rendered it somewhat less than completely desirable. Fortunately, intelligent re-engineering and judicious "off the shelf" technology have solved those problems for modern T-28 enthusiasts.

The first weakness detected in the T-28 was its brakes. Historically, military pilots had enjoyed exceptionally long runways. Although the T-28 was fitted with Goodyear disc brakes, they were inadequate for short-field landings. On the B and C models, the brakes must not only stop the plane, but help steer it, too. Civilian owners found brake wear excessive and replacing the pads time-consuming and difficult.

A simple, low-cost solution was discovered in Cleveland brakes, which were originally designed for the Beechcraft QueenAir. The Cleveland brakes feature an external disc with pads that present more than twice the surface area of the original Goodyears. Switching to Cleveland brakes has improved a weak point at reasonable cost without detracting from the T-28's appearance. The bolt-on modification now available includes new wheels.

Another weak point, and one of the biggest knocks against the T-28, was its radial engine, which leaked vast quantities of oil. Consequently, the T-28 was considered a "dirty" airplane. At airshows, owners used to spend an inordinate amount of time cleaning their planes. That task alone dis-

couraged many potential T-28 buyers and frustrated its owners.

The best solution to the oil leaks was designed and engineered by Dave Clinton of Darton International in the mid-1980s. Dave flew F-4s for the Navy in Vietnam and owned a P-51 until he sold it in the early eighties. Unable to live without a warbird, Dave picked up a T-28 at a good price. On his first flight, he and his wife set out to deliver some Christmas presents. The day was blustery and she was wearing a white suit. When Dave fired up the engine, the gusty cross wind blew the engine's initial "blow off" straight into the cockpit, and his wife emerged looking like a Dalmatian. That irate spouse was all the impetus Dave needed to solve the T-28's leaky oil problem.

After some research, Clinton found the T-28A's Pratt and Whitney engine had a rocker cover retrieval system that kept excess oil out of the valve rocker arm covers during engine operation. This system was not installed on the more powerful 1820 engines, which had been installed in the T-28B and C models. Clinton

The right console contains the electrical functions. Important items of note include the starter and primer buttons and the unique control shift switch. Below the console are the circuit breakers.

FINAL TOUR OF DUTY

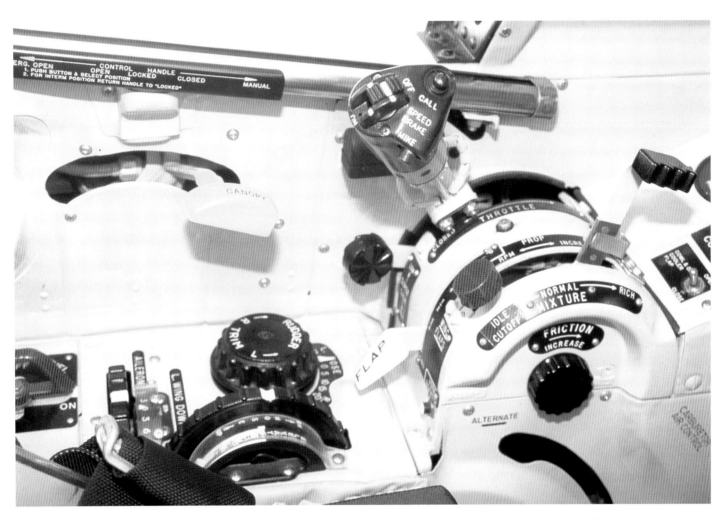

The throttle quadrant on B and D models is the same as on this C model. Throttle, supercharger, flaps, propeller and mixture controls are arranged logically for easy location, eliminating the need to actually look down in the cockpit. The yellow handle actuates the canopy.

NORTH AMERICAN'S T-28 TROJANS

had limited success in his first attempt to install his own rocker retrieval system. He then added an oil shut-off system, which helped some, but the central problem persisted. So did he.

When he installed a pumping system, ninety percent of the problem was solved. Aiming higher, Clinton designed a static scavenge drain system that removes all the waste oil from the lowest cylinders, draining it through an electrically controlled valve into a scupper can, which is pressurized to pressure-evacuate any collected oil through the engine breather system. Dave claims his solution was the result of applied engineering, not an original design.

The cowl flaps and the door on the oil cooler are activated by a switch on the left console.

Intended only for his personal aircraft, Clinton at first had no intention of marketing his technology. But as he traveled in his T-28, owners of other T-28s began leaving business cards and notes on Clinton's airplane asking how he kept it so clean. After building a few kits for other T-28 owners, Clinton marketed it as the Clean Kit®. This modification alone enhanced the T-28's popularity and increased the joy of T-28 ownership. At the Oshkosh fly-in over the past few years, it has been easy to spot the few T-28s without Clean Kits®—they all have oil puddles under their engines and black streaks down the sides of their fuselages.

The last of the few weaknesses of the T-28 design is its propeller. Model A owners have been replacing its standard, two-bladed propeller with a three-blade version. However, B, C and D models with their 1820 engines and three-bladed propellers also have propeller problems. Many of their propellers fail inspections, and serviceable replacement propellers are increasingly rare and expensive.

Once again Clinton came up with a solution. Clinton's goal was to find a replacement prop at a reasonable cost that equaled the original propeller in performance and appearance. He investigated and tested S2F Tracker blades. The S2F was a carrier-based antisubmarine warfare plane that was equipped with two 1820 engines, and there is a surplus of S2F blades that can be modified for T-28 use. The modified S2 propeller exceeded Clinton's expectations.

These three improvements, as well as other small ones, have enhanced the value and overall enjoyment of the T-28. Today's T-28s look and perform better than ever. Just as a new Harley looks like an old one, today's T-28s have few of the old quirks and problems, yet all of the plane's legendary sounds and style.

The small nose wheel was specified on all Navy aircraft.

CHAPTER 1

T-28A: GOOD-BYE TAIL DRAGGER, HELLO A-MODEL

Trainers have never played the glamour roles of fighters or attack aircraft. Instead, they are trusty work horses that get used and abused. Trainers must be relatively easy to fly, with no bad habits, and most of all, they must be forgiving. A trainer should be easy enough for a new pilot to fly, but present some challenge to more experienced pilots so they can make a smooth transition into higher performance aircraft.

Many U.S. companies have built military trainers, but the most respected builder was North American Aviation. By the end of World War II, more than fifteen thousand Air Force T-6s and Navy SNJs had been produced by North American as trainers. Pilots who won the war flying everything from P-51s

Though slightly blurred by its rotation, the width of the blade is visible on this T-28A's Aero Products two-bladed propeller. The triangular structure behind the pilot is a roll-over pylon, which was built into only the first half of A models produced.

This colorful paint scheme was commonplace at Edward's Air Force Base Test Pilot School. The standard two-bladed propeller has been replaced by a Hamilton Standard 23D40 three-bladed prop. The large nose wheel and nose wheel steering are common on all A models. (photo Joe Cupido)

NORTH AMERICAN'S T-28 TROJANS

The markings on this A model were typical of the early fifties—a silver fuselage and gray exhaust strip—and the tail insignia denotes the U.S. Army Airborne Electronics and Special Warfare Board. This particular aircraft was rescued from an aviation trade school. Previously, it had been assigned to Pope Air Force Base, Fort Bragg, North Carolina, to photograph equipment drops.

to B-29s, learned their basic flight skills in these sturdy trainers.

Following the war, the T-6 stayed in the Air Force inventory as a trainer, but its days were numbered. Tail draggers had become a thing of the past.

FINAL TOUR OF DUTY

The paint scheme on this A model is typical of the Air Force: fluorescent orange on natural metal with "U.S. Air Force" written in large, block letters along the fuselage. This view shows the mass of the roll-over pylon and the reason for its removal: poor visibility from the rear cockpit.

Tricycle landing gear allowed higher landing speeds. Besides, the jet age had begun.

In 1947, the U.S. Air Force issued specifications for a new trainer. At that time, the Air Force was flying F-80s, F-84s and F-86s. The specifications for

NORTH AMERICAN'S T-28 TROJANS

Notice the speed brake, which is usually found on the T-28, is absent on this stout A model. The speed brake was originally designed for the A model, and was installed on two prototypes, but never made production. The wrinkled skin above and rearward of the baggage hatch reveals the weakest area of the fuselage. The kink in the trailing edge of the right wing, however, is an optical illusion produced by the canopy of the aircraft from which the photo was taken.

FINAL TOUR OF DUTY

The Aero Products propeller has a service life of 2,000 hours and finding a serviceable one is a rarity. Removal of the propeller is a challenge, because it is secured with a special nine-notch nut torqued to 1,200 foot pounds.

the new trainer asked for an aircraft that would provide a platform with the flight characteristics of the jets of that era. It called for tricycle landing gear, tandem seating and an all-metal, low-wing construction. The engine would be the 800 HP R-1300 Wright Cyclone. Although lightly powered, it was low weight and easily maintained.

NORTH AMERICAN'S T-28 TROJANS

A design characteristic of the T-28 is its easy maintenance. The cowlings are easily unlatched and propped open with a curved rod that is stored inside the cowling. The open cowling reveals the R-1300-A Wright Cyclone 800 HP engine. This angle also gives a good view of the replacement Hamilton Standard three-bladed propeller, which had originally been used on the DeHaviland Otter. T-28 owners have reported an increase in acceleration and cruise performance with the use of this prop.

North American Aviation and Douglas Aircraft both submitted proposals for the new trainer. The Douglas proposal, however, called for an aircraft with mid-engine configuration, and the Air Force felt this design would be a maintenance nightmare. As a result, the Douglas design never went beyond the proposal stage. In May 1948, the Air Force announced its selection of the North American pro-

FINAL TOUR OF DUTY

posal and ordered two prototypes, designated XBT-28. On September 26, 1949, the first XBT-28 flew. According to the specifications, it was a low-wing, all-metal design, powered by the Wright Cyclone air-cooled radial engine. Its tandem seating was covered by a two-piece bubble canopy. It had the required tricycle landing gear with a steerable nose wheel. Both prototypes had an under-fuselage speed brake that was not on the production A models. Flight characteristics were superb: a top speed of 292 MPH and a ceiling of 31,000 feet. After flight tests were completed, the Air Force ordered 266 aircraft, which were designated T-28A.

The smooth underside just forward of the baggage door is where the missing speed brake is normally attached. The large baggage door is hinged in the front and has two latches in the rear.

NORTH AMERICAN'S T-28 TROJANS

In April 1950, the Air Force took delivery of its first production models. Once outfitted with the required military radios and navigation equipment, the T-28's weight rose, slightly deteriorating its performance. Though the T-28 Trojan was well-received by pilots and ground maintenance crews, its only major flaw was its engine. One design concept had been to simulate jet performance, and the jets of the early fifties were sluggish at low speeds. So was the A model.

Several changes were made during the production run between 1950 and 1953. The most visible modification was the removal of the rollover pylon with a subsequent reduction in canopy height. The pylon had hindered visibility from the rear seat, and the lower canopy improved the plane's side profile immensely. Two additional 26-gallon tanks were mounted outboard of the main tanks, bringing the total fuel capacity to

The T-28, designed for easy ground-level maintenance, features large clam-shell cowling.

FINAL TOUR OF DUTY

177 gallons and increasing the T-28's range to 1,175 miles.

The T-28A could be fitted with several underwing arms packages. Two different gun pods could be mounted: one contained a single .50-caliber machine gun, the other held two .30-caliber machine guns. The leading edge of the left wing contained a port and mounts for a gun camera, and underwing racks could also be hung for bombs and rockets.

The service life of the T-28A trainer ran from 1950 to 1956, when it was replaced by the T-34 Mentor. The remaining A models were relegated to National Guard service where they replaced F-51s, stored at Davis-Monthan Air Force Base in Arizona or

The open left engine cowling reveals what appears to be a complex installation of tubes and airframe structure. Circular exhaust stacks exit in pairs on each side, and visible on the inside of the cowling is the cowl flap activator. The olive green container in the upper right is the oil tank.

NORTH AMERICAN'S T-28 TROJANS

they were used by the U.S. government in foreign military assistance programs. In this capacity, T-28s were sent to South Korea, Taiwan, Mexico, the Philippines, Nicaragua, Honduras, Ecuador, Bolivia, the Dominican Republic, Argentina and Cambodia.

The Cambodia T-28s caused some heartache. After Cambodia gained its independence in the midfifties, its allegiance

North American Aviation did a wonderful job displaying the controls and gauges in the T-28. All the dials and switch panels are back-lit like those in a jet fighter. Storm lights under the glare shield light the cockpit brightly. Modern additions to most warbirds have included LORAN (on top of the glare shield) and an on-board fire system (the large red knob located below the oxygen regulator).

FINAL TOUR OF DUTY

changed several times because of internal political volatility and foreign intervention. In the early sixties, while still on good terms with the United States, Cambodia had received a small shipment of T-28As complete with armament. Soon after this delivery, Cambodian loyalties switched again, leaving the United States on the other side of the fence. During this time a U.S.-supplied Cambodian T-28A shot down a USAF O-1, killing the American pilot and a Vietnamese observer. In

The T-28 is a dual-control aircraft, and the rear cockpit is a mirror image of the front cockpit. In training, the instructor pilot rides in the back seat, where visibility is excellent. The T-28 should not be flown solo from the rear seat, however, because the weight of the pilot shifts the aircraft's center of gravity too far rearward.

NORTH AMERICAN'S T-28 TROJANS

In this cockpit, only a few avionics modifications alter the look of North American's original design. The red bar running across the stick is the control lock.

FINAL TOUR OF DUTY

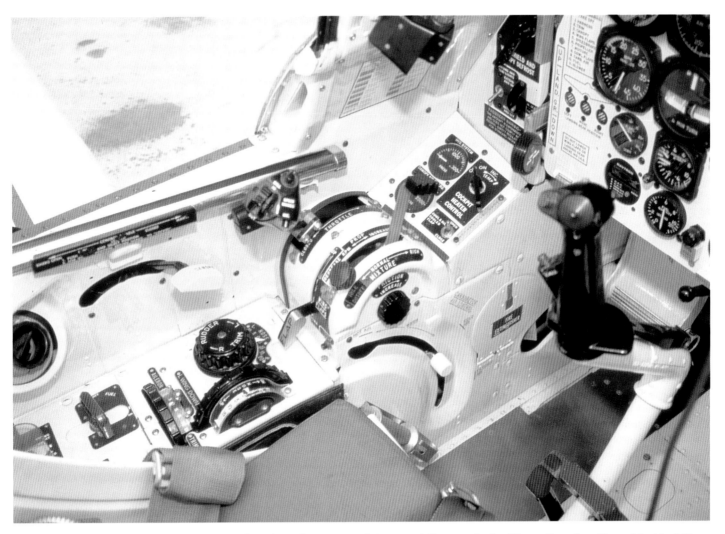

The left console on this A model contains throttle, prop, mixture and flap controls. The yellow handle set behind the throttle is the canopy control lever, and the trim controls are located below the canopy handle.

NORTH AMERICAN'S T-28 TROJANS

The A model's cowling, one flap per side, fits tightly around its seven-cylinder air-cooled engine and appears more streamlined than subsequent models with larger engines. The carburetor intake and oil cooler intake both extend back from the front of the cowling.

March 1970, another shift of Cambodian internal power allowed General Lon Nol to replace Prince Norodom Sihanouk as head of state. Lon Nol approached the United States for help in eliminating his communist enemies, and again, the United States provided aircraft—including some T-28Bs.

FINAL TOUR OF DUTY

T-28As were produced for the Air Force between 1950 and 1953, and they were last used by that service in 1959 by Air Guard units. This A model's paint scheme—silver cowling, wings and fuselage—is typical of the later models. The lower half of the fuselage was usually painted a light gray that extended from exhaust to tail. The insignia on this aircraft's tail denotes training command. The absence of a roll-over pylon shortened the T-28's canopy height by four inches, improving its looks considerably. This particular A model was awarded Reserve Grand Champion at the 1993 Oshkosh Fly-In.

NORTH AMERICAN'S T-28 TROJANS

The T-28 has a gross wing area of 268 square feet and a wing span of forty feet, one inch. Its cruising speed is 190 MPH, with a maximum speed of 283 MPH.

The T-28A story continued when the basic airframe was used by the French to build Fennecs, by the U.S. Air Force to build T-28Ds, and by the U.S. Navy to convert to T-28Cs.

Today, civilian T-28As are rarely seen and those that remain are often overlooked in favor of their more powerful siblings, the B and C models. The few civilian owners of T-28As generally make some adjustments to the original T-28 design, most often changing the propeller. The two-bladed, 10-foot diameter, hollow-steel Aero Products prop has uniformly been replaced by a Hamilton Standard 23D40 three-bladed version. The original propeller has a service life of only 2,000 hours and cannot be rebuilt. Serviceable two-bladed propellers can be found, but only at a relatively high prices. Conversion to the three-bladed unit is relatively easy and provides smoother engine operation, better acceleration and increased cruise performance. As one owner said, "I can't understand why the Air Force didn't use this propeller on the T-28A in the first place."

This neglected A model was photographed in the Ft. Rucker Aviation Museum in 1974. Its fluorescent paint has faded from exposure to the sun. The square panel in front of and below the star on the national insignia is the battery access door. (photo Joe Cupido)

NORTH AMERICAN'S T-28 TROJANS

CHAPTER 2

T28B: THE NAVY GETS ITS FIRST VERSION

During the fifties, the U.S. Navy realized that it needed to upgrade its basic training aircraft; as a tail dragger, its current trainer, the SNJ, was no longer compatible with other fleet aircraft. In 1952, the Navy evaluated two T-28As that were on loan from the Air Force, and although the A was well-liked, the Navy's main complaint was that the A model had too little power.

Therefore, the Navy asked North American to modify an A model to accept the 9-cylinder Wright Cyclone R-1820-9HD, a 1,425 HP engine. The larger engine required a new cowling, and the oil cooler intake was moved from the

From this angle, it is tough to distinguish an A from a B model T-28. The T-28 was used by all branches of the U.S. military, but this T-28 carries the markings of the U.S. Marine Corps. It was judged Best T-28 at the 1989 Oshkosh Fly-In. (photo J.J. Genat)

FINAL TOUR OF DUTY

Although the T-28 looks ungainly on the ground, it is attractive in the air. The exhaust strip and anti-glare panel are both black, and the rescue sign points to the emergency canopy opening lever.

NORTH AMERICAN'S T-28 TROJANS

Although attractive, the overall-gray paint scheme of this T-28 is not representative of authentic military markings. The owner has also added a spinner to the propeller. This particular aircraft made more than 15,000 landings between April 1967 and August 1983 while in U.S. military service.

leading edge of the cowling to a location farther back. Where the A model had two exhaust stacks on each side, the B model had three. A three-bladed, 10-foot, 1-inch-diameter constant-speed propeller was also fitted. The under-fuselage speed brake, which had been deleted from the production

A model by the Air Force, was added to the Navy's new B model.

On April 6, 1953, the first T-28B flew at North American's Columbus, Ohio, plant. The project test pilot was Bob Hoover, whose reports were glowing.

FINAL TOUR OF DUTY

Beginning in December 1961, Navy training and reserve aircraft were painted Glossy White and International Orange. This aircraft is painted with VT-27's "Delta" markings.

The prototype airframe only needed the added power of its new engine to excel. The performance gains made in the T-28B were exceptional. They included a top speed of 346 MPH and a service ceiling of 37,000 feet. Between 1954 and 1955, North American built a total of 489 T-28Bs.

On final approach, with full flaps and speed brake deployed, the sink rate of a T-28 is comparable to that of a jet fighter.

The Navy T-28Bs, or Trojans, were assigned to Pensacola, Florida, and Meridian, Mississippi. When first introduced to the fleet, the T-28Bs were painted in the then-traditional glossy orange-yellow color scheme. In 1961, the Navy changed the colors to Insignia White and International Orange, high-visibility colors used on training aircraft and some reserve aircraft.

The T-28s spread throughout the fleet, serving in

FINAL TOUR OF DUTY

Glossy orange-yellow was the Navy's standard color scheme for trainer aircraft when the T-28B entered the fleet. Late in 1961, the colors were changed to orange and white.

a multitude of roles. One of the most common was base hack, an aircraft assigned to a base of operations (NAS or NAF), but not to a specific squadron. Hack T-28s were used typically by the base commander or by other command-level officers for transportation and to maintain their flying skills. Most hacks carried the orange and white color scheme of the training command or a modified version of it.

NORTH AMERICAN'S T-28 TROJANS

With the exception of two avionics modifications (an ARGUS 5000 moving map and the Foster LORAN), this cockpit is laid out as North American originally intended. The buttons on the stick are marked "B" for bombs and "R" for rockets.

The T-28s also served throughout the fleet as drone controllers, test pilot school aircraft and as observation planes at the Navy parachute facility. In addition, both the Army and Air Force began to use B models, painting over the Navy markings and adding their own service identification. In 1961, a small group of Bs was modified, strengthening their wings and adding another hard point for armament. Eventually, these modified planes would be the first T-28Bs to see combat.

FINAL TOUR OF DUTY

A view from the rear seat during a tail chase shows the excellent visibility from a T-28 cockpit. The red knob in the lower left allows the rear-seat passenger to stop the canopy movement in an emergency. The container on top of the glare shield is a first-aid kit.

Eight T-28B Trojans, along with some Douglas B-26Bs, were the first U.S. combat aircraft to arrive in Southeast Asia, landing at Tan Son Nhut in late 1961 as part of the Farm Gate detachment. Although the Geneva agreement of 1954 prohibited jet aircraft in Vietnam, the Farm Gate crews were in the country ostensibly to train their Vietnamese counterparts. Any T-28 tactical missions had to take place with Vietnamese backseaters. America's direct involvement began on December 26, 1961,

NORTH AMERICAN'S T-28 TROJANS

Student pilots flew from the front seat during normal training exercises. During instrument training, the student sat in the rear seat with an instrument flying hood pulled over his head that was attached to the instrument panel. The hood stows behind the rear seat, as seen here. (photo Joe Cupido)

when two T-28s flown by U.S. pilots conducted a strike mission.

During that same month, fifteen T-28Bs were delivered to the Second Fighter Squadron of the Vietnamese Air Force at Nha Trang. These Trojans replaced aging F8F Bearcats. The first Vietnamese Air Force T-28 combat loss occurred on June 13, 1962, when one was hit by ground fire on a bombing run. The first U.S. pilot rescued by helicopter in

FINAL TOUR OF DUTY

The T-28's large canopy allows a pilot easy access to the cockpit. The front and rear sections of the canopy are connected and move as one unit, and is normally operated by a hydraulic system. The canopy can also be opened manually using an external lever on the front of the rear canopy frame. Pressure from an internal air bottle snaps the canopy open in an emergency.

NORTH AMERICAN'S T-28 TROJANS

Between 1954 and 1955, the Navy took delivery of nearly 500 T-28Bs, which were assigned to training squadrons in Pensacola, Florida, and Meridian, Mississippi. The color scheme of this B model is representative of aircraft assigned to Pensacola in 1976.

Vietnam was Capt. E.C. Meek, shot down September 10, 1963, while flying a T-28. The B models in Southeast Asia were eventually replaced by D models. T-28Bs were last used by the military in 1984 to train Navy student pilots.

Since then, most B models have ended up with warbird enthusiasts, but there have been two other

FINAL TOUR OF DUTY

non-military users of note. The first was the National Science Foundation for a 1966 project called Hail Swath. The NSF needed an aircraft sturdy and reliable enough to penetrate thunderstorms and hailstorms, and it preferred a reciprocating engine to a jet because of the jet's tendency to ingest ice. The NSF determined that a single engine was adequate, because with twin engines, if you lost one, you'd

Normal cruise speed for a B model is 170 knots with a maximum altitude of 37,000 feet. Overall length is thirty-two feet, eleven inches. This beautifully restored B model was awarded Grand Champion Warbird at the 1992 EAA Oshkosh Fly-In.

This T-28 is starting to generate lift, as evidenced by the extended oleos. The aircraft takes flight between 85 and 90 knots.

Behind this Hamilton Standard propeller is a Wright 1820 nine-cylinder engine. The exhaust panel on the side of the cowl is stainless steel. The T-28's 1820 engine and fuselage were difficult to keep clean until the invention of the Clean Kit®.

FINAL TOUR OF DUTY

The foresight of North American Aviation's engineers is evident in the strength of the T-28's landing gear. Originally designed for

long, paved runways, this gear was able to withstand the rigors of carrier landings after a few minor modifications. This B model has a large nose wheel, whereas most Navy T-28s had a smaller nose wheel. The small light on each strut is a gear position light, which is activated when the wheels

are down and locked and the external master lights are on.

NORTH AMERICAN'S T-28 TROJANS

The exhaust path extends the full length of the fuselage, and tight canopy and baggage door seals are essential to prevent toxic fumes from entering the cockpit. It's not uncommon for a canopy to creep slightly open during flight, and most owners frequently tap the canopy control to the closed position—just to make sure.

probably lose the other, too. Furthermore, a slower, propeller-driven aircraft would need less armor plate to survive the hail impacts. The first choice of the National Science Foundation was the World War II SDB Dauntless dive bomber. The T-28 came in second. However, since T-28s were plentiful and inex-

This T-28B has just landed and is taxiing in with its cowl flaps and oil cooler door open. The two-piece canopy is also fully open, providing fresh air to the pilots. The green tinted area on the top of the canopy is an additional piece of Plexiglas that was added to Navy aircraft assigned to bases in the southern states.

pensive, ultimately they were selected over the scarce and costly SBDs.

The first T-28B went to Project Hail Swath in 1967, its leading edges covered by .09-inch-thick aluminum plating. The front of its cowling was plat-

Many fleet T-28s were painted light gull-gray with a white underside, with black anti-glare shield and exhaust strip. All B models were outfitted with the shorter canopy. This B model was awarded Grand National Champion Warbird at the 1988 EAA Oshkosh Fly-In.

ed with .125-inch-thick aluminum, and the bubble canopy was replaced by a framed canopy with flat acrylic sheets. All this additional armor plating added only 700 pounds to the aircraft. A variety of instrumentation was also added, with the wing hard points serving as sensor mounts. Between 1970

FINAL TOUR OF DUTY

A hard break to the right reveals the speed brake on the underside of this B model. A speed brake was an additional flight control added to fighter jet aircraft of the era, and was different from the dive brake found on WWII dive bombers. The dive brake was used to control speed during a dive on a bombing run.

and 1980, the T-28 penetrated more than 750 storms and masses of data were collected. Although struck by lightning several times, the T-28 prevailed. Its only accident occurred on a slippery runway, which damaged the prop and engine.

The T-28B was also used by the Alaska Division of Forestry, which in 1984 received seven T-28Bs at

This T-28's light gray paint scheme blends into the scattered clouds below. An aircraft carrier is barely visible through the clouds.

no cost. The T-28B's mission was fire detection and to serve as lead aircraft for firefighting aircraft—a forest-fire forward air controller! One of the Alaska modifications included an infrared camera and a video camera, so video images could be transmitted in real-time to the fire boss at a ground station. The

FINAL TOUR OF DUTY

With the advent of Darton International's Clean Kit®, today's T-28 is clean and tidy.

five operational T-28Bs in Alaska averaged 150 to 300 flight hours per year. In the early nineties, these T-28s were phased out in favor of more modern twin-engine aircraft.

NORTH AMERICAN'S T-28 TROJANS

Total flap area is more than fifty-three square feet. Large flaps and two footholds (the black squares) provide easy access to the top of the wing. On the left side of the fuselage are footholds to access the cockpit.

A B model banks away.

FINAL TOUR OF DUTY

Main landing gear struts are strong enough to make a carrier landing or to take the abuse of student pilots practicing touch-and-gos. T-28s were originally equipped with Goodyear brakes, which today have been replaced by Cleveland brakes such as those used on the QueenAir. Cleveland brakes are less costly, easier to work on and provide greater stopping power. Note the red paint on the inside edge of the landing gear doors. In flight, any door not fully closed is easily spotted.

The T-28 was the last military aircraft designed with a single radial engine. When restorations like this one are displayed at airshows, they attract swarms of naval aviators who trained in T-28s. Affection for this aircraft is evident on the smiling faces of these aviators, who approach the T-28 as if she were a long-lost sweetheart.

NORTH AMERICAN'S T-28 TROJANS

CHAPTER 3

T-28C: TROJAN WITH A TAILHOOK

The Navy was delighted with the performance of its T-28B Trojans, and in an attempt to limit its training models to a single aircraft type, it asked North American Aviation to develop what turned out to be the C model of the T-28 for use on its aircraft carriers.

North American modified a B-model airframe to withstand the pounding that carrier landings would inflict on the airframe. The rear fuselage was redesigned and strengthened, and the lower rear fuselage and rudder were notched to allow the addition of a tailhook. The notching meant that the tail skid had to move forward. The valving and travel of the landing gear struts

During a section-takeoff maneuver, two aircraft rotate simultaneously. The takeoff roll starts with an exaggerated head nod from the lead pilot. After reaching flying speed, the lead aircraft rotates quickly followed by his wing man. Gear-up is signaled in one of two ways. The lead pilot can either give a thumbs-up or simply raise his gear. Full retraction of the landing gear takes a little over six seconds.

Although we were not given permission to land, we enjoyed our flight past one of the Navy's newest nuclear aircraft carriers, the USS Abraham Lincoln. T-28Cs were used to teach naval aviators how to land on aircraft carriers. At that time, two carriers were stationed in the Gulf of Mexico for that purpose. The marshalling pattern for aircraft due to make a carrier landing is with the tailhook down.

NORTH AMERICAN'S T-28 TROJANS

The red rocks of Arizona provide an stunning backdrop for a T-28C marked in the Navy colors of VA-122.

were also stiffened to handle the abusive landings better.

Adding the hook, its hydraulic retraction mecha-nism and the structural modifications needed to counteract the severity of carrier landings, increas-ed the plane's weight only slightly. However, the increased weight and a smaller diameter propeller

FINAL TOUR OF DUTY

Today, owners paint their names and rank (if former military) or call signs on the sides of their canopies. On this T-28, the rear seat area is highlighted by the letters GIB, which stands for "Guy In Back."

(9 feet, 4 inches for the C versus 10 feet, 1 inch for the B) reduced the C's performance somewhat. The smaller diameter propeller was necessary for carrier landings to prevent it from digging into the deck when the hook grabbed the arresting wire.

The C prototype made its first flight on September 19, 1955. After a short period of testing by the

FINAL TOUR OF DUTY

Navy, production on the T-28C began. Between 1955 and 1957, North American produced 299 T-28Cs and converted a number of As and Bs to C specifications.

Like previous A and B models, all Cs were designed to handle underwing stores. A number of Cs were modified with strengthened wings and an additional hard point on each wing to handle fighter-bomber roles. Several of these Cs ended up in Vietnam with the South Vietnamese air force and in other areas of conflict around the world. On these Cs, the tail hooks were removed and the lower rear fuselage was faired over.

The cockpit of the C is the same as that of the B, except for the tailhook handle on the right side of the front cockpit. Its operation is

One trend of today's T-28 restoration enthusiast is to paint the plane dark blue, similar to World War II and Korean War-era Navy aircraft. Although actual use of the dark blue paint scheme in the fleet was minimal, it looks great today. This particular aircraft had been modified by North American for a combat role in Zaire. The tailhook and related hardware had been removed and the opening was faired over. Several T-28Cs were also modified in this way for use in Vietnam.

simple: Push the lever down, and the hook goes down. Also, the landing checklist placard now included a fourth instruction: "Check Hook."

One item unique to the C model is its cowling strakes, horizontal aluminum strips that were bolted to the length of the cowling just below the cowl flaps and above the exhaust. The strakes were added to C models to aid in spin recovery while carrying wing stores. They had no effect on stall characteristics or stall speed.

Imagine the thrill of landing on an aircraft carrier for the first time. T-28Cs provided that thrill for many new naval aviators. Prior to landing on the boat, however, each student pilot had to complete Field Carrier Landing Practice (FLCP), or "bouncing." Aided by an Landing Signal Officer (LSO) stationed on the ground, the student pilot is monitored every step of the way on his approach. The LSO is in constant radio communication with the pilot and calls out small corrections to ensure a smooth, measured descent.

The pilot controls his approach with the help of the "meatball," a mirror-lens system on the runway that enables the pilot to monitor his glide path on approach. The standard carrier approach in a T-28 is at a speed of 82 knots. Proper landing technique at that time required that the main gear touch first with the nose wheel about one foot off the deck.

Kill markings on the canopy of this C model reflect the friendly rivalry between warbird owners.

The nose wheel is then lowered. When bouncing, upon touchdown the pilot applies power and takes off again, then the pilot re-enters the pattern for another attempt.

FINAL TOUR OF DUTY

Between 1955 and 1957, North American Aviation produced 299 T-28Cs for the Navy. These aircraft represented a milestone in the flying careers of many young aviators: their first arrested carrier landing.

The term "bouncing" comes from this series of quick approaches, touch downs and takeoffs where the plane seems to bounce off the runway. If at any time on any approach the student pilot is "out of

This C model looks as though it has a few extra wheels, but hidden behind it is another T-28.

shape," the LSO waves him off according to carrier landing rules. Occasionally, the LSO may wave off a perfect approach to simulate a foul deck condition, just to keep a student on his toes. Following this

FINAL TOUR OF DUTY

exercise, the student and LSO conduct an extensive debrief to discuss each approach. Safety is paramount when you're flying 8,000 pounds of aluminum low and slow.

Once a student pilot has shown an aptitude for carrier landing, he gets to fly out to the boat. This is the day a naval aviator never forgets—carrier qualification, also known as CQ or "carequals." Anybody can land on 5,000 feet of wide, firm, concrete, but it takes someone special to

Cowling strakes extend from the front of the cowling rearward above the exhaust. Strakes were installed on C models with gun packages or external stores to aid in spin recovery. The scoop below the exhaust is the oil cooler and cockpit air intake. The small scoop on the top of the cowling in front of the windscreen pulls in air for magneto cooling.

catch the three-wire on a pitching carrier deck moving at 25 to 30 knots. At that time, all T-28 carrier

qualifications took place in the Gulf of Mexico aboard two carriers: the *USS Antietam* (CVB-36) and the *USS Lexington* (ATV-16). To qualify, a student pilot had to complete two touch-and-gos and four arrested landings with subsequent deck launches. For safety reasons, flights to the boat were made in sections. Upon reaching the boat, the lead pilot made radio contact with the carrier and waited for permission to land. Of course, waiting was not what these young aviators wanted. Waiting meant marshaling at 2,000 to 3,000 feet, an altitude from which the carrier landing area looked mighty small. Waiting also meant pondering the task at hand.

Excellent airmanship and a strong frame enabled this T-28C to survive an engine failure and subsequent gear-up landing in a Wyoming field in 1991. After it was repaired, it won Best T-28 at the 1993 Oshkosh EAA Fly-In.

FINAL TOUR OF DUTY

NORTH AMERICAN'S T-28 TROJANS

The wing span of this T-28C is forty feet, one inch, and its height is twelve feet, eight and one-half inches. The propeller is nine feet, four inches in diameter, six inches smaller than the B model. This reduction in diameter was intended to add additional propeller clearance to accommodate carrier landings.

The initial approach to the carrier pattern was made in echelon right formation with hooks lowered. Part of being a naval aviator is flying a tight, hot formation into the break. At about mid-deck, the lead aircraft breaks left, followed by each subsequent aircraft in the flight at 10-second intervals. Power is cut back to 15 inches of manifold pressure, cowl flaps and oil cooler door are opened as the pilot enters the turn at a 45-degree angle of bank. When the airspeed drops to 140 knots, the

Two T-28Cs chug along in formation.

flaps and wheels are lowered. The speed brake is deployed, the pilot's harness is locked and the canopy opened. The downwind portion of the approach is at 82 knots at an altitude of 325 feet, and parallel to the ship on a line 1,000 to 1,200 feet away.

Upon reaching a point abeam the LSO's position on deck, the approach turn begins. This 180-degree turn is done at a 20-degree angle of bank. At approximately 90 degrees in his turn, the pilot visually picks up the mirror-lens (meatball), and verbally indicates that he sees the meatball to the LSO by

NORTH AMERICAN'S T-28 TROJANS

"calling the ball." Keeping the ball in sight, the pilot sets power to 26 inches of manifold pressure and starts a descent varying in glide slope rate from 350 to 500 feet per minute.

The pilot's eyes are fixed on the ball as he flies the plane down to the deck. When the cut light flashes, he cuts power and only now looks at the landing area of the deck. The next sensation after touchdown should be the rapid deceleration of the plane caused by the hook grabbing the wire, the resultant force pushing the pilot forward against the shoulder harness. If there is no deceleration, one of the four arresting wires was missed in what is called a "bolter." The pilot must then apply maximum power and retract the speed brake to take off and re-enter the pattern for another landing attempt. A successful trap, however, leaves no time for celebration. The pilot's eyes scan the deck for a yellow shirt to

The obvious feature that distinguishes T-28Cs from all other models is the addition of a tailhook. To accommodate the hook, the bottom edges of the fin and rudder were trimmed, as was a portion of the rear fuselage, and the tail skid was moved forward. Once installed, the tailhook is lowered by gravity and bungee pressure and is retracted using hydraulic pressure. Black and white stripes painted along the length of the hook make it more visible to the LSO during carrier landings.

FINAL TOUR OF DUTY

direct him in clearing the deck for the plane behind him.

On take-offs, the T-28 could be catapulted from a carrier, but it was usually just flown off the deck. During take-off,

Proper configuration for a carrier landings calls for everything to hang out except the kitchen sink. For safety reasons, carrier landings were made with the aircraft's canopy open. Flying with an open canopy is not difficult, although the noise level increases and the front-seater is buffeted by a small amount of wind. However, as you can see, the occupant in the rear must hold on to his hat.

NORTH AMERICAN'S T-28 TROJANS

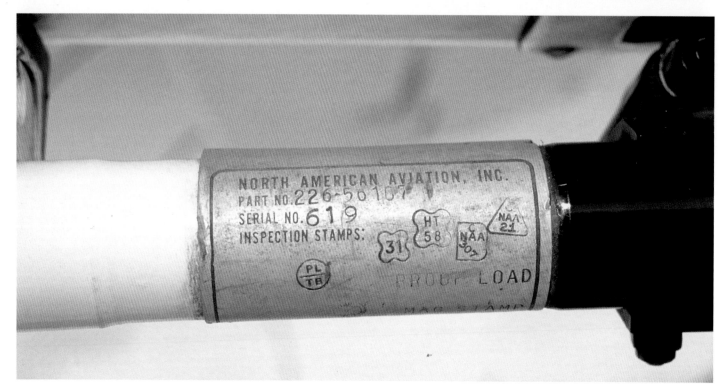

Tailhook inspection stamps on a T-28C.

required aircraft configuration called for an open canopy, full flaps and 8 degrees of right rudder trim. Once lined up, the yellow shirt responsible for take-off gives the student the turn-up signal. The pilot then advances power to 30 inches of manifold pressure, with the brakes held tight. After a quick scan of the instruments, a sharp hand salute or head nod

from the pilot to the launch officer means "ready for launch." If the deck is clear, the launch officer kneels down, touches the deck and points to the open end of the deck. The pilot releases brakes and increases power to 52.5 inches of manifold pressure. Some rudder control is necessary for directional stability. Once elevator controls are attained, the

Award-winning aircraft are as immaculate on the inside as they are on the outside. This is the cockpit of the C model selected as Best T-28 at Oshkosh in 1991. The lever on the right operates the tail hook.

NORTH AMERICAN'S T-28 TROJANS

These two photos (above and right) are of the same aircraft before and after restoration. Early in the restoration process it was a combination of bare aluminum, the faded original U.S. Navy International Orange and dirty Insignia White. This T-28C last saw Navy duty in VT-6 where it was the commanding officer's aircraft. The number 600 written below the cockpit denotes it as the first (double zero or "double nuts") in the series of aircraft assigned to the squadron and flown by the CO. Restoration began from the inside out: Under the unpainted cowling is an immaculately detailed 1820 engine. Restoration complete, the T-28 flies over the Salton Sea in the Southern California desert. The quality of the restoration was acknowledged with an award for the Best T-28 at Oshkosh in 1991.

FINAL TOUR OF DUTY

pilot raises the nose, and the T-28 flies off the deck. The pilot quickly retracts the aircraft's wheels, and releases the flaps at an altitude of 300 feet with 100 knots of airspeed. Finally, the canopy is closed, and the pilot is flying again.

T-28Cs offered thousands of naval aviators one of the most memorable events of their lives: carrier qualifications. It taught them the skills they needed to advance to A-4s, A-7s, F-4s, or F-14s. Today's T-28Cs no longer land on aircraft carriers, but they still provide their owners with hours of enjoyment.

The T-28C was replaced for Navy carrier qualifications by the T-2 Buckeye, another product of North American Aviation, which began production in 1958. One aviator who flew both said, "There's a lot of T-28 in the T-2. The T-2 flies like a fast T-28."

CHAPTER 4

FENNEC: WORLD TRAVELER T-28

uring the mid-fifties, France was entangled in a colonial war. France's conflict in Southeast Asia had turned into a losing proposition and a similar situation was developing in Algeria. Insurgents were rising up in Algeria, but France was determined to quell the disturbance. The French Air Force was sent in to support ground troops with North American T-6s. The French had been using T-6s since 1957 in more than twenty light support squadrons. The T-6s, which had been equipped with machine guns, rocket launchers and armor plating, were inexpensive and easy to maintain, but were also slow and vulnerable to ground fire. In late 1959, the French government began to search for a replacement for the T-6, but had no French aircraft in production that could be modified to suit its needs.

The French government determined that the T-28B would be a wonderful replacement for its T-6s, in part because of its 1,425 HP engine. They wanted a faster

A cowling graphic depicts a small desert fox, known as a Fennec. The fox's large ears act as a cooling system in the intense desert heat, not unlike the cowling flaps on a T-28.

FINAL TOUR OF DUTY

This Fennec was probably the first T-28 to fire a shot in anger. Following two prototypes, this aircraft was Fennec number one in production. It served with two French squadrons in Algeria, 3/09 and 3/04.

airplane. However, the U.S. Navy had priority on the production of North American's B models, so a suit- able alternative was needed. The United States offered France 148 surplus A models from Davis-

Although the Fennec was not painted in this manner when used in combat, the camouflage paint scheme looks attractive today.

Monthan's mothball fleet, which was in storage in Arizona.

During this period, Pacific Airmotive of Burbank, California, had obtained the rights to produce a civil-

FINAL TOUR OF DUTY

Specifications for the Fennec did not include a speed brake. This Fennec has been modified with the installation of a bolt-on speed brake.

ian T-28 variant. Pacific Airmotive had begun to buy surplus T-28As, adding a larger engine and market-ing them as Nomads. Because of this T-28 experi-ence, the French selected Pacific Airmotive to per-

A modified instrument panel with updated avionics is installed in this Fennec. The lever on the stick engages the nose-wheel steering, and direction is determined by applying pressure to the rudder pedals.

FINAL TOUR OF DUTY

The markings on this aircraft's tail designate it as a T-28F, the common designation for the Fennec in the United States. In France, the Fennec's designation was T-28S.

form modifications to their specifications and to produce documentation manuals on their newly acquired A models.

The first French/Pacific Airmotive prototype was re-engined with a Wright R-1820-76A, of B-17 vintage, and fitted with the Hamilton Standard three-bladed propeller. The cowlings were B-type sheet metal with one exception—an air scoop was added to the top of the cowling to provide additional cock-

NORTH AMERICAN'S T-28 TROJANS

Exhaust streaking is evident, even on the dark coloring of this Fennec. This photo was shot moments after rotation, just prior to retracting the gear.

pit air, which would satisfy the increased ventilation needs of desert operations. Armament and armor plate were also added. The prototype aircraft (#51-3593) and three modified T-28A airframes were shipped to Sud Aviation in St. Nazaire, France, in early 1960. Although the prototype aircraft was destroyed in an accident on April 16, 1960, Sud Aviation continued to modify T-28 aircraft, which were re-designated by France as the T-28S Fennec.

A T-28 Fennec soars over Palm Springs, California.

Combat-ready T-28S Fennecs offered several armament capabilities. The wings were modified to accept two hard points each. Each internal mount was designed to carry one of the following: a machine gun pod with two guns of 12.7 MM, a 120-kilogram bomb, a 260-kilogram bomb with short tails, a rocket pod with 7X68 MM rockets or a rocket pod with 36X37 MM rockets. Each outboard pylon could carry a 120-kilogram bomb, a 260-kilogram bomb, a special Secan type 51 bomb, a rocket pod

NORTH AMERICAN'S T-28 TROJANS

Fennecs inherited nose-wheel steering from the original A model. This Fennec has the smaller nose wheel of the B model.

with 7X88 mm rockets, a rocket pod with 36X37 mm rockets or a single rocket of 105 mm or 120 mm. The French called the rocket pods "bee's nests."

FINAL TOUR OF DUTY

The Fennec color scheme was natural metal or silver overall with a black anti-glare panel and exhaust stripe. The red, white and blue French rondel insignia was painted on the wings. Its tail sported a small, rectangular French flag of vertical bars in red, white and blue. Below that appeared the original U.S. Air Force serial number, followed by the Fennec serial in smaller, black numbers. About two-thirds of the Fennecs featured higher canopies with rollover pylons. The speed brake was not included in Sud's modification.

By mid-1961, more than 100 combat-ready Fennecs were spread among four light attack squadrons stationed in Algeria. Not long after the French reached full strength, the conflict wound down, and by the end of 1962, T-28 operations in Algeria had ceased. Operational losses were light, with only twenty-three total aircraft lost to combat or accidents. Many Fennecs were returned to France for training and reserve squadron use. Eventually, the Fennecs would be scattered all over the world. In 1965, twenty-five Fennecs were sold to Morocco; and in 1966, forty-six were sent to Argentina. By 1967, the French had stopped using them, but continued to sell off their remaining Fennecs.

NORTH AMERICAN'S T-28 TROJANS

Fennecs can be found with either the original high canopy and roll-over pylon or with the lower canopy of the late A model. The canopy on the white Fennec in the foreground has been cut down an additional four inches in height. The dark blue Fennec in the background still has the standard low canopy.

Argentina was the largest, single beneficiary of French Fennecs, receiving sixty-three, which were used by both the Argentine air force and navy. The Argentine navy's modified version of the Fennec, designated T-28P, included underwing pylons altered to accept air-to-surface missiles for antishipping patrols. In addition, approximately twenty of the T-28Ps were fitted with tailhooks. The tailhooks were not the elegant installations of North American's C models, instead they were simply bolted to the bottoms of the aircraft with the business end resting against the tail skid. Argentina eventually sold nine of their Fennecs to Uruguay.

FINAL TOUR OF DUTY

T-28s were never equipped with propeller spinners, but many owners have added them. This particular aircraft was the test bed for Darton International's Clean Kit. This Fennec won best T-28 at Oshkosh in both 1987 and 1994.

The twenty-five Fennecs sold to Morocco in 1965 were used during border flare-ups with Algeria. In the late sixties, Morocco sold nine Fennecs without armament to Haiti. The Haitian air force installed .50-caliber machine guns on the inboard pylon.

About twenty of the French Fennecs that had been retired from service were sold to private American owners. France also sold one to China and one to Formosa, and there are numerous stories of the passage of Fennecs in small numbers to other Third-World republics. The few Fennecs that remained in France were used for maintenance training.

The United State's designation of the Fennec is T-

NORTH AMERICAN'S T-28 TROJANS

This Fennec (#68) saw action with two French squadrons, 3/05 and 4/37. Prior to its import to the United States in 1971, it had logged only 4,000 hours of total flight time.

28F. Most U.S. Fennecs flying today have been brought up to B model standards by adding a speed brake and updating the controls back to the standard North American convention. Most Fennecs have lost the extra cockpit ventilation scoop.

One way to spot a Fennec is by the two battery-access doors on the left side of the fuselage. On the Fennec and the B models, the battery door is located at the leading edge of the horizontal stabilizer.

(In A models a forward battery is located just rearward of the end of the canopy.) Because of the Fennec's larger engine, a few components were shifted to maintain a proper center of gravity. Although each aircraft has assumed a new personality with each new owner, even under new paint and updated avionics, Fennecs still remain the first T-28s that went to war.

FINAL TOUR OF DUTY

NORTH AMERICAN'S T-28 TROJANS

CHAPTER 5

T-28D: WE CALLED 'EM TANGOS

The T-28D was the last military variant of the T-28 built. It came in two versions, a Dash-5 and a Dash-10. T-28Ds, or more specifically AT-28s (the A denoted "attack"), were built for combat in Southeast Asia. The B and C models were being retired and the lessons learned from their tours of duty provided the knowledge to re-engineer the T-28 into the D models.

The first D models, D-5s, were rebuilt A models. North American delivered 191 T-28D-5s; and Fairchild Aviation, 50. The 800 HP engine was replaced with an 1820 and B/C cowlings. Armor plate and self-sealing fuel tanks were added. The wing spars were strengthened, with each wing receiving three hard points and a .50-caliber gun. Another seventy-two D-10s, all of

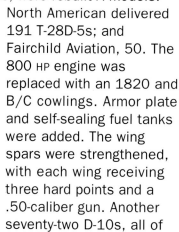

T-28D-5s were built from A models that had originally been manufactured without speed brakes. When reworked into D models, the speed brake was added.

which were origi-
nally B models,
were eventually
built by Fairchild.

A unique feature
of the T-28D was
its extraction
seat. This was an
improvement over
the previous
method of aban-
doning an aircraft
in flight that was
recommended on
the As, Bs, and
Cs: Diving out of
the cockpit toward
the trailing edge of
the right wing.
Limitations to this
bailout method
were speed (you
had to be moving
slower than 120
knots) and alti-
tude. Dangers
included the possi-
bility of smacking
into the horizontal
stabilizer.

The markings of the 4077 combat training squadron, active in the early sixties, adorn this T-28D. This aircraft began as an A and was modified with the appropriate D-level hardware.

NORTH AMERICAN'S T-28 TROJANS

The T-28 extraction seat or "Yankee Extraction Seat" was originally developed for the Douglas A-1 Skyraider. It had zero-zero capability, which meant you could sit in the aircraft on the runway and punch out at zero airspeed, zero altitude. The seat featured a solid-propellant rocket. Pulling the handle activated a detonation cord, commonly called a det cord, that blew away the Plexiglas in the canopy. Ejection was initiated with the canopy closed, otherwise you'd hit the frame on the way out.

In the rear seat of this T-28 sits Virassak "Sak" Pradichit, who had been a Vietnam-era T-28 pilot with the Royal Laotian Air Force and had flown more than 2,500 combat missions.

FINAL TOUR OF DUTY

NORTH AMERICAN'S T-28 TROJANS

The cowl insignia of the U.S. Air Force Air Commandos says it all: "Any Time, Any Place."

I asked former Raven FAC Craig Morrison how he was checked out in the extraction seat's use. Morrison recalled that his training consisted of a lieutenant's telling him: "This hooks to this, and that hooks to that, and if you need to get out, pull this handle and it will blow you through the canopy and everything will be fine!" Morrison never took the E-ticket ride, but everyone had the greatest faith in the system. "I saw one guy bail out long after I thought he should," he recalls. "The neatest part was that as soon as he was out, his chute was open. The airplane just kinda disappeared from underneath his feet."

In 1966, this T-28D-5, the fourth production model, was converted from an A model into the Dash-5 format at the North American facility in Columbus, Ohio. It was then shipped to Udorn, Thailand, and from there, sent to join the fray in Laos. In 1988, the airplane was dismantled and shipped out of Laos in huge crates. When unpacked for restoration, more than 50 patched bullet holes were discovered. (photo Joe Cupido)

The D model replaced aging Bs and Cs in combat. The most interesting and best documentation of T-28Ds in combat is in Christopher Robbins's book, *The Ravens*, which chronicles the secret U.S. war in Laos. A small group of American pilots went to Laos as part of what was known as the Steve Canyon Program. U.S. pilots went in as advisors to train Laotian pilots and to act as forward air control

The T-28 is fully aerobatic, however, negative G flight is limited to no more than ten seconds. The airframe is rated at plus 4.5 Gs and minus 2 Gs, but stock T-28 engine installations do not provide for negative G lubrication. (photo Joe Cupido)

(FAC) for U.S. Air Force aircraft flying out of Thailand and Vietnam. As in Vietnam, Laotian backseaters were supposed to fly with the U.S. Air Force pilots. Military formalities were minimal, since officially, these guys didn't exist. They were known simply as The Ravens.

FINAL TOUR OF DUTY

Anyone who denies the T-28 warbird status should read about the exploits of the Ravens in Laos. Along with O-1s, the Ravens flew T-28s, which they called "Tangos." (photo Joe Cupido)

Most of these pilots had not flown the T-28 before and they never used the name "Trojan." Instead, they called their Ds "Tangos," which is the military alphabet word for the letter T. Training was minimal too, especially if the pilot to be checked out already had flight experience. Captain Morrison's T-28 train-

ing spanned three days. A captain by rank and a combat tactics instructor, he presumably was one step ahead of the young lieutenants already there, but according to Captain Morrison, he didn't feel that way. He went to Udorn, Thailand, on a Friday, walked in and said he was there to get checked out

NORTH AMERICAN'S T-28 TROJANS

FINAL TOUR OF DUTY

on the T-28. A guy said, "Okay, here's the Dash-1," and pointed to a plane out on the ramp. Seeking out a T-28D that sat in the hangar to avoid the 100-degree heat, Captain Morrison sat in the cockpit, looked at the book, went through the checklist and thought, "Well, fine, if I can figure out how to start this thing, I can probably fly it." Soon, an Air Force lieutenant came out and said, "Let's go flying."

Flight number one consisted of a walk-around, then a short flight with touch-and-gos, stalls and spins. Saturday morning they did aerobatics, and Saturday afternoon was devoted to instrument flying under the hood. Sunday morning the plane was loaded with practice bombs. Sunday afternoon, they loaded up with rockets and practiced strafing. What

was Captain Morrison doing Monday morning? He was a full-fledged T-28 combat pilot.

During the brief training, the young lieutenant-instructor decided to show Captain Morrison something about torque in the T-28. The point of his demo was to illustrate the torque reaction in a simulation of "going around." The gear and flaps are down and you're about to flare when somebody says "go around." The demo, performed at 5,000 feet, went like this: Captain Morrison had the stick and rudder, the lieutenant controlled the throttle. When the lieutenant firewalled it, all that sudden torque rolled the airplane three-quarters onto its back. Therefore, Morrison learned, the first thing you do on a go-around in a T-28 is to start feeding in rudder, adding power until you can't control it any more, then hold the throttle steady. This maneuver served as a transition training device for pilots coming out of jets where rudder use is minimal except in some air combat maneuvers.

Captain Morrison earned a Silver Star during a combat mission in a T-28, thanks to its renowned sturdiness. FACs were normally not shot at from the ground, the logic being that the enemy would give away their position. But once a FAC marked an enemy position, he became a target—a choice one. One day Morrison was escorting A-1s in and out of a cloud-covered valley in a T-28. Just as he rolled to re-mark a position for the A-1s, he was caught in

NORTH AMERICAN'S T-28 TROJANS

As this AT-28D-10 steps up, you can see the .50-caliber gun mount and three hard points on each wing. This D model, a survivor from the Royal Laotian Air Force, was selected as the Judges' Choice at Oshkosh, 1994. (photo Joe Cupido)

FINAL TOUR OF DUTY

When restoring this T-28, the owner fitted it with a pair of D-model wings and then finished it in the colors of the U.S. Air Force 4400th Combat Crew Training Squadron of Elgin Air Force Base. The T-28Ds from that squadron were some of the first D models in Vietnam. This beautiful restoration has won several awards, including Best T-28 at Oshkosh, 1992. (photo J.J. Genat)

the crossfire of two 17.7mm guns opening up from an adjoining hill. He took several hits that did serious damage to his engine and blew the top off one cylinder. "I flew that sucker thirty or forty miles in the mountains on eight out of nine cylinders escorted by a couple of A-1s," Morrison recalls.

NORTH AMERICAN'S T-28 TROJANS

Originally a flat gray, this D model has been freshly painted in the tri-color camouflage of the U.S. Air Force 4407th combat training squadron of the First Special Operations Wing, which was based at Hurlbert Field, Florida, in the late sixties. (photo Joe Cupido)

In fact, not only was the one cylinder inoperative, it was gone. Captain Morrison found out later from a mechanic that in an adjacent cylinder a push rod had been creased by another bullet. The mechanic

The inverted triangles on the side of the fuselage below the cockpit warn the ground crew of the presence of a pyrotechnic device that was used to extract pilots from the plane in an emergency: the Yankee Extraction Seat. Pilots who flew T-28s in combat had great faith in the extraction seat because it worked so well. (photo Joe Cupido)

showed Morrison that if the push rod had broken, the 1820 would not have run on seven cylinders and he would have had to bail out. Morrison took that piece of metal, and with no force at all, broke the

rod. He realized then just how close he had been to becoming a POW. Summing up his feelings about the T-28, Morrison states, "I loved that airplane! It saved my life."

The T-28s were also used by several other countries, including Vietnam and Laos. The U.S. T-28s in Laos were shared with the Royal Laotian Air Force, and an informal agreement allowed The Ravens to use perhaps two of the fifteen or so on the ramp. Airplanes rotated in and out, so rather than flying a specific airplane, the pilots worked with a variety of airplanes. The T-28s of each MR (military region) were either marked or had no markings. The RLAF (Royal Laotian Air Force) displayed their Erewan symbol, which showed three elephants, on the fuselage. Surrounding the Laotian symbol was a three-sided

This is a pilot's view of a well-worn AT-28D-10 cockpit that had once belonged to the Royal Laotian Air Force. Notice the additional armor plates bolted to the floor. This aircraft will one day be fully restored.

FINAL TOUR OF DUTY

frame into which you could slide a square panel carrying any other insignia. The Laotian marking could also be covered with a blank panel. The Ravens generally flew unmarked.

Royal Laotian Air Force pilots flew numbers of missions far in excess of what would be considered high among American pilots. Royal Laotian Air Force pilots flew more than 100 missions a month, several a day, albeit brief ones. One of the most honored and legendary Royal Laotian pilots was Lee Lue, who flew more than 5,000 combat missions. A teacher in his remote mountain village, Lee Lue first flew at age 27. He completed and returned from missions thought to be impossible. His peers drove themselves to excel so as not to lose face.

Years of combat flights and many additional years of neglect have left this T-28D's throttle quadrant in sorry shape.

This is a Royal Laotian Air Force AT-28D-10 as delivered from abroad. The damage to the rear fuselage occurred in transit, but all the D models recovered from Laos showed evidence of battle damage.

Stories abound of Royal Laotian pilots who flew fifteen missions over a ten-hour time span, never leaving the cockpit. Virassak "Sak" Pradichit, a Laotian pilot with 2,500 combat missions said, "How could I get out of the cockpit with my general waiting on the ground to re-arm my plane?" The only medal Sak ever received was for saving his damaged T-28 after a mid-air collision with a fellow pilot.

When Laos fell in the mid-seventies, the T-28Ds were abandoned on an airstrip in Xieng Khong. In 1988, a deal was struck with the Laotian government to sell sixteen of the T-28Ds that had been flown by the RLAF and The Ravens.

The round emblem depicting three elephants, known as the Erewan, was painted on the side of Royal Laotian Air Force T-28s. This symbol could be hidden or changed by inserting a new panel into the three-sided frame surrounding the symbol.

NORTH AMERICAN'S T-28 TROJANS

CHAPTER 6

LOOKS LIKE A BRICK, FLIES LIKE A CADILLAC

At rest on the ramp, the T-28 looks as if it would fly like a brick, with its big blunt nose, oversize canopy and thick wing. A raving beauty, it's not. But what North American Aviation sacrificed in looks, it made up for in function. You already have some history about each model and

Proper formation flying is an efficient way to move aircraft in a group. When approaching an airport for landing, the formation switches to an echelon configuration (shown here) just prior to breaking over the field. During the break each aircraft in the echelon peels off in equally spaced increments directly over the runway. The break reduces each aircraft's speed and results in equal spacing for the downwind leg of the approach. While in the echelon formation, the lead pilot hand-signals the timing between each aircraft's break, and each pilot passes the signal down the line. The lead pilot conducts all radio communication for the flight and he must be skilled and smooth, for each movement is replicated throughout the formation.

are familiar with the T-28's unique systems, so let's find out how this ugly duckling flies.

We got together recently with some former military pilots and some warbird owners and compared notes on how the T-28 stacks up against other aircraft that are often revered as the icons of air combat.

Here's what they said about the T-28 versus the P-51. First of all, the P-51 is a marvelous airplane, probably the most efficient warbird a civilian can own. The Mustang has a high-speed laminar wing, a short, coupled airframe and a long thrust axis.

A flight helmet is de rigueur for today's warbird pilot. The helmet is fitted with a boom mike, headphones and oxygen mask receptacles—graphics are optional. The pilot also wears a Nomex flight suit, for fire protection, and strapped onto the pilot's back is a sport-type parachute. Just visible on the bulkhead behind the pilot is a fire extinguisher. The instructions given by virtually all T-28 owners to rear seat passengers prior to takeoff go something like, "If we have an engine failure, we will probably ride it down; if we have a fire, we will probably bail out." The NATOPS manual states: "Rear seat pilot dives forcibly toward trailing edge of wing. The front seat pilot should roll onto the wing." Bailout is recommended off the right side where prop wash reduces the danger of striking the horizontal stabilizer.

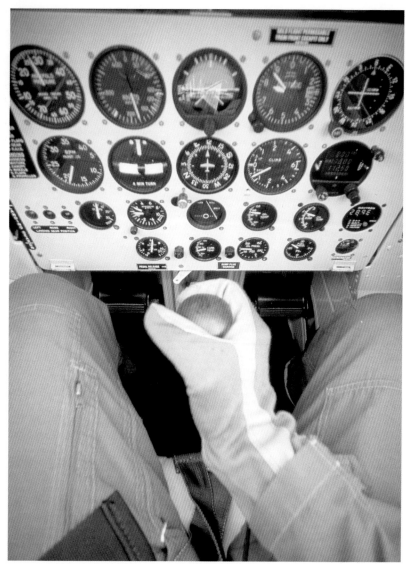

Because of its hot performance, a Mustang can get a relatively inexperienced pilot into trouble quicker and more seriously than a T-28 can. Remember though, the Mustang was a fighter not a trainer. From the standpoint of flyability, the Mustang lacks the control harmony of the T-28. You have to fly the P-51 more purposefully, always aware that little things can upset the Mustang, the rudders have one pressure, the elevators another, and the ailerons a third. The Mustang is also less neutrally stable, like most fighters. The Mustang will spin inverted, the T-28 won't.

A few years ago, a comparison test was conducted in an attempt to settle once and for all which World War II aircraft was best. The aircraft chosen for the test were a P-51, a P-47, a F6F Hellcat and a F4U Corsair. They were evaluated as a test pilot would have evaluated them on ground handling, visibility, cockpit layout, dogfighting, tracking, turning, accelerating, acceleration in a 1-G pushover, climbing rate and so on. The pace plane for the test was a T-28.

When flying in formation, a pilot scans the instruments. The instrument panel on this T-28 is not laid out in standard military configuration.

FINAL TOUR OF DUTY

The T-28 was not being compared officially, but such observations naturally occurred during the evaluation. The only warbird that could outclimb the T-28 was the F6F Hellcat. In the dive, the T-28 stayed with the P-51 to the T-28's redline. The T-28 had the best roll rate. For the dogfight sequence, the T-28 was the target airplane. Every time the P-51 tried to track the T-28 through a level 4-G turn, the Mustang slipped out. True, the T-28 is a more modern airplane, and you might expect better performance with successive designs, but it makes a great story when a T-28 cleans a P-51's clock.

Warbird owners describe the T-28 as a real Cadillac in its handling. The whole craft is designed around its engine. It certainly doesn't fly like it looks, stubby and chunky, not at all pretty on the ground, and it doesn't sound too good, either. But in the air, it's a thoroughbred. Drive a Mustang, a T-6 or a T-34 above 200 to 250 knots, and their controls get very heavy. Take a T-28 out to the redline and you can still fly it with two fingers, just as if you had serve-boosted controls. It's a sweet-flying airplane.

Parking a T-28 no longer means leaving a large oil stain on the ramp. Installation of a specialty engine kit has eliminated one of the major objections to T-28 ownership: messy oil leaks.

While fully restoring a T-28, the fuselage is propped on rotisserie-style supports. The entire fuselage can be rotated easily, making even the most difficult locations accessible.

The T-28 in formation flying? Compared to any warbird in formation flying, the T-28 gets high marks. The T-28 almost equals a jet airplane's formation performance. Its other fine qualities include predictability, control harmony and good engine response, making the T-28 a fine formation flyer. Because the T-28 is heavy, it accelerates fairly slowly in formation. It has plenty of power, but when

FINAL TOUR OF DUTY

This formation of T-28s is led by a Fennec, followed by B and C models, respectively.

you do add power, it takes a while before anything much happens. Same at the other end of the spectrum; due to its weight momentum, it takes a massive power reduction to slow the thing down. Once in motion, though, the T-28 eats up the sky.

What's best about the T-28? Well, the best is also the worst: It's almost too easy to fly. Take up an amateur and in an hour, he thinks he's Sierra Hotel—it's such an ego grabber. The T-28 provides plenty of automation to mask mistakes. An inexperienced pilot might mismanage the engine during low-

NORTH AMERICAN'S T-28 TROJANS

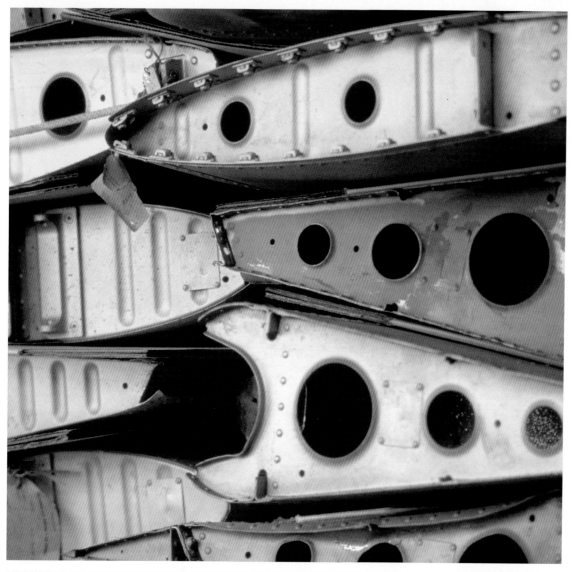

level aerobatics or get caught off guard by the T-28's high sink rates. In the traffic pattern, the T-28 comes down at 2,000 to 3,000 feet per minute on final approach, which can seem pretty exciting. If your landing speed is too slow, you won't have the thrust energy to flare properly. A pilot who has never flown a high-sink airplane would doubtless be surprised. It's hard to perceive that sink rate at 500 feet, but down to 200 the T-28 feels like it's *really* coming

The restoration enthusiast's friend: a pile of spare parts.

FINAL TOUR OF DUTY

Several aircraft restorers specialize in the T-28. The hangar at Pride Aircraft in Rockford, Illinois, is filled with T-28 projects in various stages of completion.

NORTH AMERICAN'S T-28 TROJANS

Each engine carries a metal tag identifying its manufacturer and other mil-spec data. Shown is a manufacturer tag on an 1820 engine.

This is a Hamilton Standard decal on a B model's propeller.

FINAL TOUR OF DUTY

down. And if your air speed is too low, that is not where you want to be. But come in at 100 or 110 knots and it's a piece of cake. The T-28 is a wonderful spot landing airplane—it comes right down and doesn't float.

The factor that warbird owners love most about their T-28s

Depicted are the many colors of today's T-28s.

NORTH AMERICAN'S T-28 TROJANS

The lead T-28B still retains much of the original Navy orange and white paint scheme. On the wing, the C model has been restored in Navy colors.

FINAL TOUR OF DUTY

A normal field take-off requires no flaps. For a short field take-off, half flaps are recommended, as we see here. Carrier take-offs required full flaps.

is that they can be shared. If you buy a jet, you can't have company. With any single seater, you can't share rides. Also, the T-28 is a terrific cross-country airplane with plenty of baggage space. Best of all, its owners love to call up a fellow pilot and say, "Hey, you wanna come out and play?"

NORTH AMERICAN'S T-28 TROJANS

This C model spent part of its Navy career as an instrument trainer at NAS Corpus Christi, Texas, and it has logged only 3,500 total hours.

FINAL TOUR OF DUTY

A tight echelon formation is led by a C model with two French Fennecs on its wing.

NORTH AMERICAN'S T-28 TROJANS

Two T-28s wing across the Midwest.

FINAL TOUR OF DUTY

Flying formation in a T-28 affords the pilot and his passenger many beautiful sights, such as the late afternoon view of this C model.

NORTH AMERICAN'S T-28 TROJANS

A T-28 owner's dream: a perfectly preserved B model. This orange and white T-28B is a former Navy craft that was acquired by the Army. The Davis-Monthan storage facility in Arizona provides an excellent environment where aircraft are cocooned and preserved for extended storage. All the aircraft's openings are covered to prevent birds and insects from nesting, and the canopy is covered to limit damage to the Plexiglas in the hot desert sun. The tubes curling out of the canopy frame vent pressure from heat build-up inside the fuselage.

FINAL TOUR OF DUTY

A FINAL WORD OF THANKS...

Many people merit extra recognition for helping me with this book. First, thank you Ron Lee, you introduced me to the T-28. Ron flew me from California to Oshkosh in his T-28B—a trip I will never forget.

Special appreciation and thanks to two of the most knowledge-able T-28 owners in the country, John Harrison and Dave Clinton. They developed and conduct (under the auspices of Darton International in Carlsbad, California) a one-of-a-kind, intensive, five-day course on the workings of this marvelous aircraft. Dave invented the Clean Kit® and other accessories that make owning a T-28 much less work than before and much more fun.

Thanks, Dave, for the ride of my life in a dogfight with an F-4F Wildcat in the skies over Illinois. John Harrison is the evangelist of the T-28, always willing to teach and counsel fellow owners or enthusiasts like me. The way John flies a T-28, you would swear he was assembled right into the airframe at North American.

Thanks to John Morgan who, with his band of experts at Pride Aircraft in Rockford, Illinois, does the finest T-28 restorations. Whenever I asked for a favor, Morgan said yes. Thank you Herb Baker, of Baker Restorations, for letting me photograph your shop and the work in progress. Herb also gave me the inside scoop on the

Ravens and their T-28 mission in Laos. Speaking of Ravens, a smart salute to Craig Morrison (Raven 20) and Virassak "Sak" Pradichit (RLAF) for their thoughts on the T-28 in combat. I'd like to thank Commander Mike Babin, *USS Abraham Lincoln,* and Lieutenant Commander John Brindley, public affairs officer, NAS North Island, for their cooperation and assistance in arranging our fly-by over the *USS Abraham Lincoln.*

Thanks to these T-28 owners who donated seat-time to me.

Dr. Ralph Glasser	T-28B/D
Dave Clinton	T-28 Fennec
Bill Montague	T-28C
Bill Scully	T-28 Fennec
Steve Scott	T-28A
John Harrison	T-28B
Al Grant	T-28C
Ron Lee	T-28B
John Shoffner	T-28 Fennec
Larry Gayler	T-28B
John Morgan	T-28B

Jacob Mast	T-28C
Dan Lawson	T-28C
Bill Sullivan	T-28D
Neil Weaver/Ben Scott	AT-28D-10
Brian Kenney	AT-28D-5
Harlow James	T-28B
Robert Beranger	T-28B
Lud Corrao	T-28C
Bill Jones	T-28C
Dr. Rich Sugden	T-28C

Thanks to the following T-28 owners for their assistance:

Dick Ervin	T-28A
Les Salz	T-28B

And finally, many thanks to Kathy and Stoney Stonich for their help and enthusiasm. They are the heart and soul of the North American Trainers Association (NATA).

FINAL TOUR OF DUTY